NOTES TO SELF

TIPS AND REMINDERS FOR WRITERS

First published in 2019 by Five Lanes Press
Contact: info@fivelanespress.com

Contact: author@jennyalexander.co.uk
Website: www.jennyalexander.co.uk

ISBN: Paperback: 978-1-910300-30-5

Cover and layouts: Rachel Lawston, www.lawstondesign.com

The quotation from Joy Harjo's memoir, *Crazy Brave,* is included by kind permission of her publisher, WW Norton and Company, New York. The quotation from Brenda Ueland's book, *If You Want to Write,* is included by kind permission of her publisher, Jeffery Corrick, New York.

I am grateful to these generous writers, both new to writing and old hands, who read the manuscript of this book and gave me the benefit of their feedback:

Amelia Thorogood, Laura Quigley, John Lugo-Treble, Julie Newman, Jackie Taylor, Lynne Benton, Penny Dolan, Cheryl Nosworthy, Miriam Landor and Sarah Norquoy – thank you all, so much!

NOTES TO SELF

TIPS AND REMINDERS FOR WRITERS

JENNY ALEXANDER

ABOUT THIS BOOK

Writing is a joyful thing – we are social creatures and love to share our stories, thoughts, feelings and experiences – and that joy is a big incentive for learning to push through problems and deal with doubts.

Because there will be doubts: What if it isn't good enough? What if no one wants to read it?

Of course, doubts can be part of the creative process, a kind of quality control. When they are, they should help you by flagging up real flaws and problems with your work in progress, so you know what needs doing, or by simply giving you pause so you can come back to it from a different angle.

But nine times out of ten, writers' doubts have nothing whatsoever to do with the quality of their writing; the problem lies in personal fears and insecurities, triggered by the adventure, and a lack of clarity about how the creative mind works.

Early in my writing career, whenever I stumbled across a little insight that helped me push through my own many doubts and anxieties, I would write it on a scrap of coloured cardboard and stick it on my study wall.

I still have occasional crises in confidence, I think virtually all writers do, and then I have to remind myself of the more constructive and realistic thoughts that have helped me let go of self-sabotaging ones in the past.

The brief insights and reminders in this book are not

in any particular order although they are loosely grouped thematically. You could read it all in one go or look at one or two sections a day; you could keep it on the corner of your table and dip into it whenever you need a boost.

Agree with it, argue with it, make it your own. Jot down your own ideas in the margins – the white space is for you. Be creative!

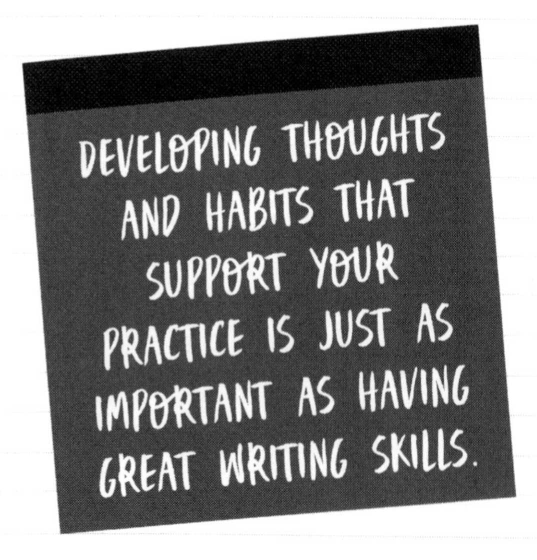

You could put that on a postit and stick it on your wall!

START NOW

Lots of people say they would like to do some writing when they have more time, but life doesn't work like that. You have to make time.

A friend who was a teacher used to get up at five in the morning and write before work. I wrote my first books in the two hours a day when my children were at playgroup, or in the middle of the night during the school holidays.

If you can find time to write just 500 words a day, which is less than two pages of A4, you'd have a novel in six months.

I find that thought encouraging!

NOTHING YOU WRITE IS EVER WASTED

Nothing you write is ever wasted, because everything you write develops you as a writer. Every note, journal entry, draft and manuscript keeps your creative energy flowing, sows the seeds of new ideas and deepens your understanding of the writing craft.

Therefore, even if something you have written gets turned down by publishers or agents it hasn't been a waste of time because it's added to the sum of your writing experience. (In fact, rejected MSS will often go on to have their day – they're eminently recyclable)

And it doesn't just develop you as a writer. Nothing you write is wasted because writing develops you as a person, increasing your self-awareness and empathy, heightening your senses and helping you develop a more creative approach to life.

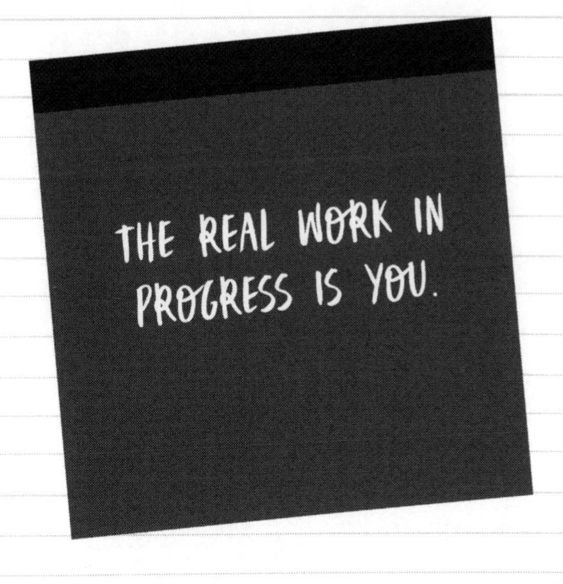
THE REAL WORK IN
PROGRESS IS YOU.

DON'T WORRY ABOUT BEING A 'PROPER WRITER'

Years ago, I was on a Society of Authors retreat at Totleigh Barton, the Arvon centre in Devon. It wasn't a taught course, but an opportunity to explore our writing ambitions as a group and with individual tutors.

The group was made up of successful authors from every area of writing – medical books, soft porn, children's fiction, educational books, poetry...

Without exception – well, except me, because I wanted to have a go at poetry – they all harboured a secret ambition to write a literary novel. They said they wouldn't feel like a proper writer unless they could achieve it.

I was struck by this hierarchical view of writing. It seemed as sensible as saying you're not a proper runner until you win a marathon. Some runners are sprinters!

If you don't think writing short stories, children's books, medical journals or whatever is being a proper writer, change your way of thinking.

YOU WON'T PLEASE EVERYONE - DON'T TRY!

Write what you enjoy writing. That is the surest way to find your authentic voice. Not everyone will love your work, but then, you don't love everyone else's.

We're all different and all of us, including publishers and agents, enjoy different kinds of books and writing styles. One editor's 'I didn't find the main character engaging' is another one's, 'I loved the young protagonist.'*

If you get rejections, don't take it personally. Ditto if you get some bad reviews.

* Actual feedback from publishers about my Young Adult novel, *Drift*.

TRUST YOUR CREATIVE INSTINCTS

The great American writer, Henry Miller, said an artist was someone who had antennae, and knew how to 'hook up to the cosmos.' The elements that make up a poem or novel or any work of art, he said, are already in the air, waiting to be given voice, and that explains why themes and discoveries tend to break at the same time in different parts of the world.

Publishers may ask for more of what's currently selling, but they're always on the look out for the next big thing and they don't know what that will be. No one predicted the mega success of *Harry Potter* or *Fifty Shades*.

Creative people are always imagining forward, past the limits of what is known. So follow your instincts and write what fires you, because you might be tapping into something that's about to fire a lot of other people too.

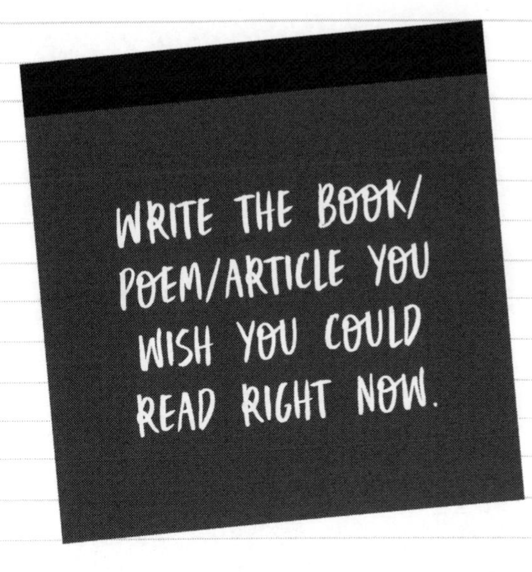
WRITE THE BOOK/
POEM/ARTICLE YOU
WISH YOU COULD
READ RIGHT NOW.

YOU ARE GOING TO HAVE ROCKY TIMES - THAT'S OK

Georges Simenon famously said that writing was not a profession but 'a vocation of unhappiness', and that isn't surprising.

Being a writer is psychologically demanding. It means:

- Spending long periods alone
- Facing huge competition
- Having an unpredictable income
- Experiencing rejection
- Having to deal with criticism
- Having to deal with praise
- Having to deal with no response at all

So if you're trying to make a career as a writer and you sometimes despair, cut yourself some slack.

Like any other vocation, the hunger to write comes at a cost, but doing something you feel you were born to do is always a blessing, a coming home to the self.

GET TO GRIPS WITH THE FINANCIAL FACTS

If your plan is to try and make a career from writing, read the latest statistics from surveys by organisations such as the Authors' Licensing and Copyright Agency and the Society of Authors, and believe the statistics.

I know you won't – nobody does, because it seems implausible that the vast majority of people doing the challenging and skillful work of writing books would actually be financially better off stacking shelves in their local supermarket.

For most professional writers, writing is part of a portfolio career. Even award winning authors these days have to supplement what they earn from their books with teaching and events, or take other work that has nothing to do with their writing.

GO DOWN TO THE WELL

Lots of creative teachers talk about the importance of taking time out from your writing and doing different things, to refresh your creative energy. It's commonly called 'going down to the well.'

As little as twenty minutes away from your desk, doing a spot of gardening or having a walk, can shift your perspective and mean you come back to your writing with fresh insights.

But it's good sometimes to take a complete holiday, if you can. Ideas you've been working on at home may seem different from far away – sometimes more exciting, sometimes less. They may form up in unexpected and intriguing ways, or fall away and release you.

YOUR NEW BOOK NEEDS YOU!

If you want to be published, either traditionally or as an indie, you're going to have to do some promoting. The days when the only thing an author had to do was write are well and truly gone, in traditional as well as independent publishing.

If events such as book signings, author talks and media interviews fill you with dread, find other ways of promoting your work. Pitch articles to magazines and blogs that publish in your subject area, seek out your online writing tribes and network.

The internet is a boon for introverts, because you can engage with lots of people without leaving the comfort of your writing room.

Try to feel positive about promoting. Your book is your baby and you don't want to abandon it the minute it's born. Nurture it tenderly into the world, and go on being around for it when it's found its place and doesn't need you all the time any more.

WRITING FICTION MAKES YOU STRONGER

Plots need problems; if everyone is happy, there's no story.

So when we write fiction, we put our protagonist in a difficult situation and imagine ways he or she might try to get out of it, overcome setbacks and reach some kind of resolution.

In this way, our protagonists teach us the art of creative problem solving and give us the opportunity to experience how it feels to gain mastery over adversity and not give up.

And there's more.

The difficult situations we put our protagonists in emerge from our deep unconscious and are connected to our everyday life in the same way as dreams, although the connections may not be obvious.

One way of seeing them is to look for emotional echoes: 'My protagonist felt shocked and anxious to stumble upon a shallow grave when she was wandering through a dark wood... and, come to think of it, I felt shocked and anxious to discover something I had previously been in the dark about...'

So helping our protagonists find their way through is more than just practice at problem solving in general – it's also a way of working on our own personal dilemmas and finding solutions in imagination.

EVERYTHING WE
ACHIEVE, WE FIRST
HAVE TO BE ABLE
TO IMAGINE.

MONEY IS NOT A MEASURE OF MERIT

In the writing business, income is not a measure of your creative achievement. Securing a publishing deal with a major publisher shows you can write but the size of the advance and publicity spend is decided on projected sales, not the quality of your writing.

The people who make the decisions won't necessarily have even read the book. Their main focus will be the concept, the hook, and how your book will fit into the market.

On the downside, this means that if you get a huge advance, it doesn't show you're the new Shakespeare but, on the upside, the pitiful contract you're far more likely to be offered doesn't mean you're a second rate writer either.

LOST IS A CREATIVE SPACE

Our understanding of the outer world is limited to what we can experience through our senses and explain through our reason, but the inner world of imagination is completely without bounds.

Every path is possible, and there are no paths until we make them. Our first ventures into inner worlds may feel bewildering and even the most experienced travellers can sometimes feel lost.

Feeling lost is horrible but getting lost is good. Getting lost is an opportunity to discover somewhere completely new, and that is a definition of creativity.

IF YOU WANT TO DO CREATIVE WORK, YOU MUST BE ABLE TO TOLERATE UNCERTAINTY.

CELEBRATE!

Working on a book all the way through to publication is a huge achievement, and that calls for a celebration. Even if it's just a simple gathering of family and friends with some fizz and nibbles, always have a launch party.

If you have a publisher, ask if they would be willing to help by, for example, designing the invitations or contributing towards the drinks bill. Don't think this is cheeky. You and your publisher are a team, and they'll be delighted to know you're making an effort to help promote your new book.

A launch party isn't just fun, it's also a great opportunity to sell some books and take some photos you'll be able to use on your website and social media.

TRY THE WEATHERLY RULE

I have it from my fellow author, Liz Kessler, that our mutual friend, Lee Weatherly, likes to celebrate on delivery of a manuscript, not just on publication. Her reasoning? Because there may be a gap of eighteen months or so between delivery and publication, and most authors have moved on to writing something else by then.

We tested this theory with a bottle of bubbly on Liz's houseboat years ago, as she had just delivered a manuscript, and I've made it my rule ever since.

I'd say, as well, don't just celebrate finishing a book that's going to be published. Completing any full-length writing project is a big achievement, whether it ever gets published or not.

Done NaNoWriMo? Put that on a cake and eat it!

Note: NaNoWriMo is National Novel Writing Month, an internet based project that gets thousands of people writing full length novels during the month of November.

BE GENEROUS

Helping others to be the best writer they can be doesn't diminish your own writing achievements in any way. It just increases your pleasure when you yourself benefit from the generosity of other writers.

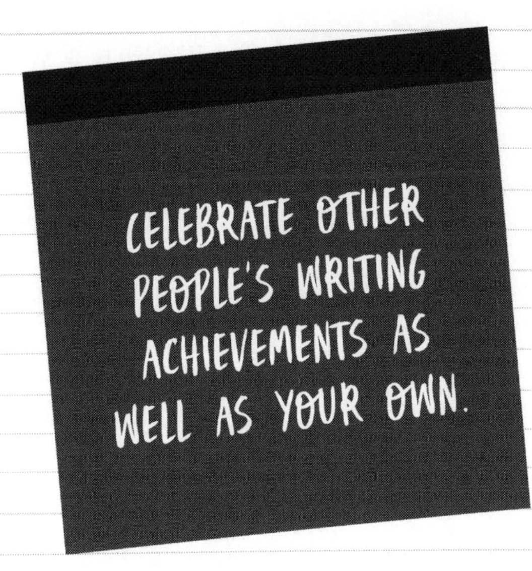
CELEBRATE OTHER
PEOPLE'S WRITING
ACHIEVEMENTS AS
WELL AS YOUR OWN.

'WHETHER YOU THINK YOU CAN, OR YOU THINK YOU CAN'T - YOU'RE RIGHT'

Henry Ford, founder of the Ford Motor Company, is one of the people who most famously said this, and it's true.

If you think you can write, you will feel enthusiastic, hopeful, motivated and optimistic about it and those feelings will help you to get started and keep going.

If you don't think you can, you will be dogged by self-doubt, and far more likely to give up.

You can choose which way you want to look at it. And you can keep renewing that choice, whenever your confidence takes a dip.

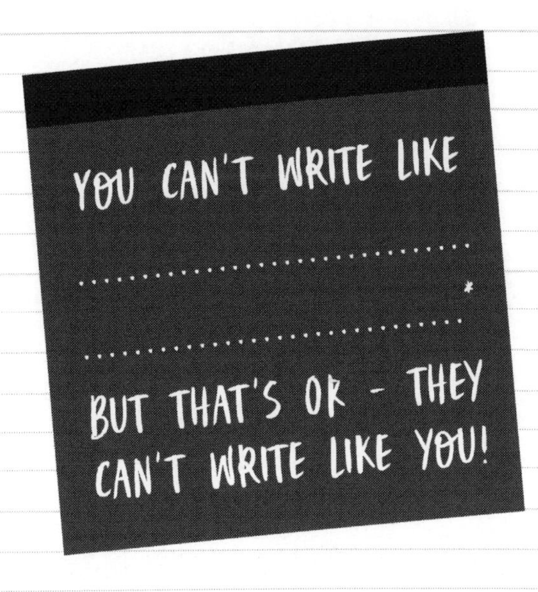

*Insert any author you personally wish you could write like

SHARE WITH CARE

Some writers like to share their work in progress with a writing group, mentor or friend – others, like me, prefer to keep it to themselves until it's the very best they can make it on their own.

Whoever you show your writing to, notice how their feedback affects you. If it makes you feel motivated and focused, full steam ahead.

If their feedback makes you feel crushed or disheartened, proceed with caution. They may not be the right writing group, mentor or friend for you.

- Writing groups need to feel safe and supportive. It only takes one person with a big ego to make group sharing potentially harmful.

- Mentors can be very helpful but that relationship can also become codependent. From time to time, check what progress you have made and how the mentoring situation makes you feel.

- Your best friend might not be your best writing buddy, not just because they may not be able to give you the most encouraging and useful feedback but also because you might be tempted to share too early. Ideas need time to firm up in the fertile darkness of your mind and if you expose them too soon they can lose their magic.

THINK WIDE

One writing project can lead on to many different publishing possibilities, and sometimes the offshoots can be where the money is.

Say you've written a novel. Could you adapt some of the story into short fiction or children's books? Could you use your research on settings and themes for some non-fiction books or magazine articles? Could you do a memoir piece on the experience of writing the novel?

If you think of yourself as only one kind of writer, you could miss out on a lot of interesting writing opportunities.

DON'T GET HUNG UP ON 'GOOD' WRITING

A lot of people who come to writing workshops express feelings of anxiety in case they won't be able to write something 'good.' I imagine this is because most of us learn to write at school, where everything is judged and graded.

Learning to identify 'good' writing at school and university completely cured me of my childhood delight in writing. But how can you say what makes 'good' writing?

I personally like a story that rattles along, with plenty of plot and not too much description, so for me Agatha Christie is a better writer than Virginia Woolf.

Seriously!

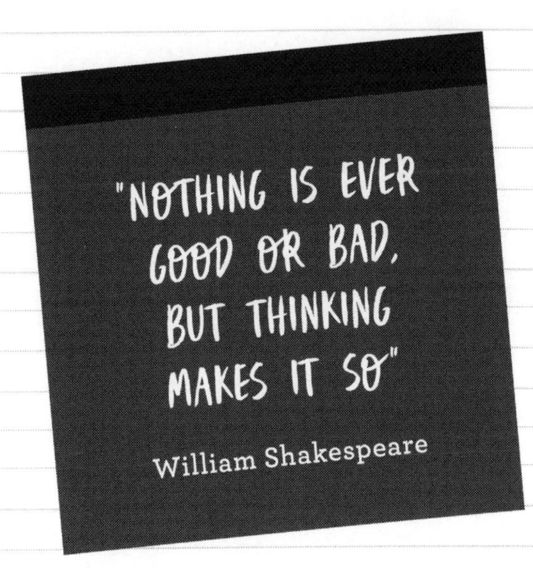
"NOTHING IS EVER
GOOD OR BAD,
BUT THINKING
MAKES IT SO"
William Shakespeare

KNOW WHAT YOU WANT

Here are six reasons why you might want to write:

- To tell your personal story
- To earn a basic living
- To get rich and famous
- To boost your profile in a non-writing career
- To get a better understanding of yourself
- For the joy of creating objects that please you

There's nothing right or wrong about these or any other writing goals, but if you aren't clear about what your personal goals are, you are much less likely to achieve them.

Most people will assume your goal is number 3, and judge your achievements accordingly. If wealth and celebrity are not major drives for you, ignore them. The only way to measure your success is in relation to your personal goals and values.

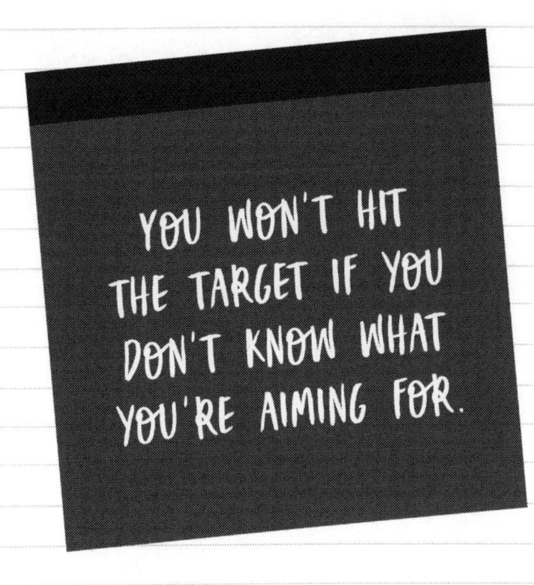
YOU WON'T HIT
THE TARGET IF YOU
DON'T KNOW WHAT
YOU'RE AIMING FOR.

WRITE DOWN YOUR WRITING GOALS

WHERE WOULD YOU LIKE TO BE WITH
YOUR WRITING IN ONE YEAR'S TIME?

IN FIVE YEARS' TIME?

IN TEN YEARS' TIME?

THE WHO, WHAT, WHERE, WHY, WHEN AND HOW OF WRITING

I once went to a writing workshop that had no structure or content – the facilitator came with only two things – a list of writing prompts and the information that to find a story all you need to do is ask the questions: who, where, when, what, why and how?

What surprised me – besides seeing someone lead a three hour workshop with no more than that – was that a lot of people in the room had never heard of finding stories by asking questions, so they were actually quite happy customers. If you haven't either, have that one on me!

WRITE WHAT YOU LIKE

I work and teach in the practice school of writing. This means instead of starting from theory and technique, you start by finding out what you want to say and getting the writing flowing.

If you write whatever you want to write, uncritically, you will enjoy it more; you will do it more often, and your writing style will improve through practice. As your skills develop, you'll be able to see what you need to learn, and that's the time to start thinking about technique.

So the first rule of writing is follow your heart. Find the ideas that fire you, enjoy writing them down and let the adventure take you where you want to go.

Don't let the critic in until you have something you like so much you will be keen to engage with the work of redrafting.

LEARNING TO FOLLOW YOUR HEART IN YOUR WRITING GIVES YOU A SKILL FOR OTHER AREAS OF YOUR LIFE.

MAKE SPACE FOR BOTH THE WRITERS IN YOU

Dorothea Brande, in her book, *Becoming a Writer* (written in the 1930s and still in print – it's that good!), says writers should think of themselves as two people: the artist and the craftsman or critic, the child and the adult.

The early stages of writing belong to the child, who must be allowed to experiment and play with words and ideas. The later stages belong to the critic.

If you let the critic in too soon, you may struggle with your first draft; if you let the child refuse to hand over her work, you may struggle with redrafting.

Just don't let them be in the same room.

'THE FIRST DRAFT OF ANYTHING IS S*IT'

Ernest Hemingway puts it so succinctly! Your first draft is not supposed to be good. The job of the first draft is simply to find out what the story is and feel your way towards the structure and voice. Making it good is the work of redrafting.

Knowing the first draft of anything is s*it should not make you feel despondent. It's something to celebrate because it sets you free.

SECOND, THIRD AND FOURTH DRAFTS CAN BE SKETCHY TOO

Redrafting isn't usually a once-and-you're-done kind of task, but a process. It's still experimental, like the first draft, but with the focus on trying to make it good.

I think of the whole process as being like making a sculpture. The ideas stage is like digging around, looking for an interesting piece of wood or stone. The first draft is choosing a piece that intrigues you and carving it down to the rough shape. The redrafting process is crafting the detail and making it beautiful.

Tip: When you're redrafting, always save your previous drafts until you're satisfied you've found your final version. Then you can play around with it to your heart's content, no worries.

GIVE YOURSELF PERMISSION TO PLAY

The early stages of the creative process can be the most challenging for us because we live in a culture that measures work in terms of productivity.

Daydreaming and playing around with ideas can feel like a waste of time, as there isn't any finished text to show for it. What's more, it doesn't feel the way we think work ought to feel.

Let go of the idea that playing is a waste of time. Value it as a vital part of your creative process.

"I LEARNED THAT YOU SHOULD FEEL WHEN WRITING, NOT LIKE LORD BYRON ON A MOUNTAIN TOP, BUT LIKE A CHILD STRINGING BEADS IN KINDERGARTEN, HAPPY, ABSORBED AND QUIETLY PUTTING ONE BEAD ON AFTER ANOTHER" *Brenda Ueland*

DON'T PANIC

When your writing is flowing, it feels amazing; when it isn't, frustration and despondency can set in.

We regard these low feelings as a problem because they challenge our cultural values. They make us antisocial in a world where naturally solitary types are labeled 'poorly socialised'; they make us still, in a world where busyness is seen as a virtue, and sad, where sadness is seen as a failure.

But solitude, stillness and emotional vulnerability are where the creative spark is kindled. What if this uncomfortable state of mind is a necessary darkness – a key to creative joy?

Hang in there.

DON'T ASK 'WHAT IS THE CAUSE?' ASK 'WHAT IS THE PURPOSE?'

When despondency stops you in your tracks, take a look at your life. Have you been trying too hard? Have you been refusing to rest? Have you emotionally over extended yourself?

If you feel disheartened about your writing, have you been trying to force it? The harder you beat your brains trying to work out how to get your story going, the more stuck you are likely to get, because creativity takes more than brainwork.

Creativity needs a spacious mind, not just a focused one. As CG Jung wrote, the creation of something new is not achieved by logic and reason but by the play instinct, following its own mysterious fascinations.

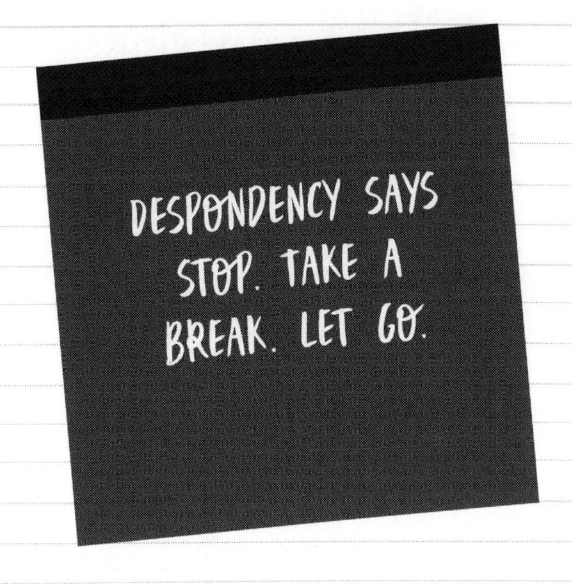
DESPONDENCY SAYS
STOP. TAKE A
BREAK. LET GO.

PUT IT ON THE BACK BURNER

Taking a break when you're stuck with your writing doesn't mean you aren't doing anything useful; it just means you're shifting your conscious focus onto something else and giving your unconscious mind the space to sort it out.

It's like when you can't remember the name of a restaurant you want to recommend, or a stand-up you've seen, or that fancy word for conjuring tricks.

Let your attention be distracted, and hey presto! Where did that come from?

MAKE WALKING PART OF YOUR PRACTICE

Walking isn't just great for your health – it shifts your attention to the wide world around you, and puts your writing in soft focus for a while.

Often, new ideas will pop into your head, so take a notepad with you or use the notes app on your mobile phone. If you need reading glasses, it might be easier to record your thoughts and write them up when you get home.

DRAW, DOODLE, PAINT OR RIP AND STICK

Delight your creative inner child with the kinds of activity that children love. When I get stuck, I might splash a bit of paint around, or lay two colours elegantly side by side on a precise dividing line. Or I'll make a collage by ripping images out of old magazines and sticking them onto a big piece of paper.

It doesn't matter what you finish up with. The point is the process, and pleasing your inner child.

If, of course, you happen to make something that pleases you, you could put that on your study wall or insights board as well.

GRAB A GLUE STICK, RIP OUT SOME WORDS+PICTURES
AND MAKE YOUR OWN LITTLE COLLAGE HERE!

'THE LIFE IS THE WORK'

An accountant said this to me, years ago, when we were discussing my tax return. While I don't believe it's a good approach for working out your tax, I do think it's a positive, holistic way of approaching your writing.

Because as soon as you start to write, whether you are published or not, you begin to see life through a writer's eyes. You notice everything. Snippets of overheard conversations; the story in a stranger's face; the movement of light in leaves. You clock people's body language and imagine how they feel inside their body, what emotions are moving through it.

That means simply strolling around or reading the paper or having a chat can be part of your writing process, even when you are not specifically pondering your work in progress.

Useful to remember if you have workaholic tendencies.

DEVELOPING A WRITER'S SENSIBILITIES ENHANCES YOUR EXPERIENCE OF EVERYDAY LIFE.

WRITE SOMETHING DIFFERENT

When one project gets stuck, writing something else can be a way of taking a break but still keeping the creative juices flowing. It doesn't need to be another big project – it could be a poem, magazine article, short story or blog post.

It could be personal writing, such as journal entries, morning pages or passages from prompts that you definitely don't intend to publish. The added bonus of personal writing is that there's absolutely no pressure on you to write well, because nobody but you will ever read it.

Everything you write keeps your creative juices flowing for when you're ready to come back to your main work in progress.

WRITE WHAT YOU KNOW

This doesn't mean, only write what you know. It means don't underestimate the value of your knowledge and experience when you're thinking about your writing.

It's easy to forget that what feels familiar to us, such as the places we've lived and the jobs we've done, is interesting and exotic to people who haven't had the same experiences.

We also tend to assume that everyone knows the things we know, because we forget there was a time before we knew them. How to look after a rabbit – I've used that in both fiction and non-fiction. How to grow vegetables. How to write.

Then there are the skills we've acquired just by dealing with life's challenges, such as cultivating happiness, building self-esteem and handling bullying. I've used all of those in fiction and non-fiction too.

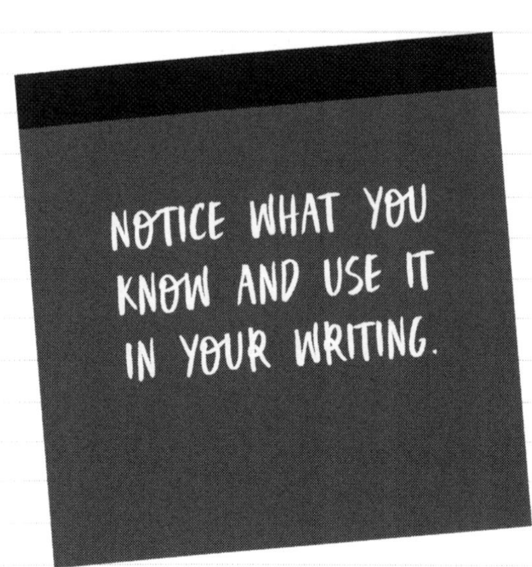
NOTICE WHAT YOU
KNOW AND USE IT
IN YOUR WRITING.

START SOME LISTS NOW AND ADD TO THEM LATER, AS MORE THINGS OCCUR TO YOU.

PLACES

HOBBIES

SOCIAL SITUATIONS

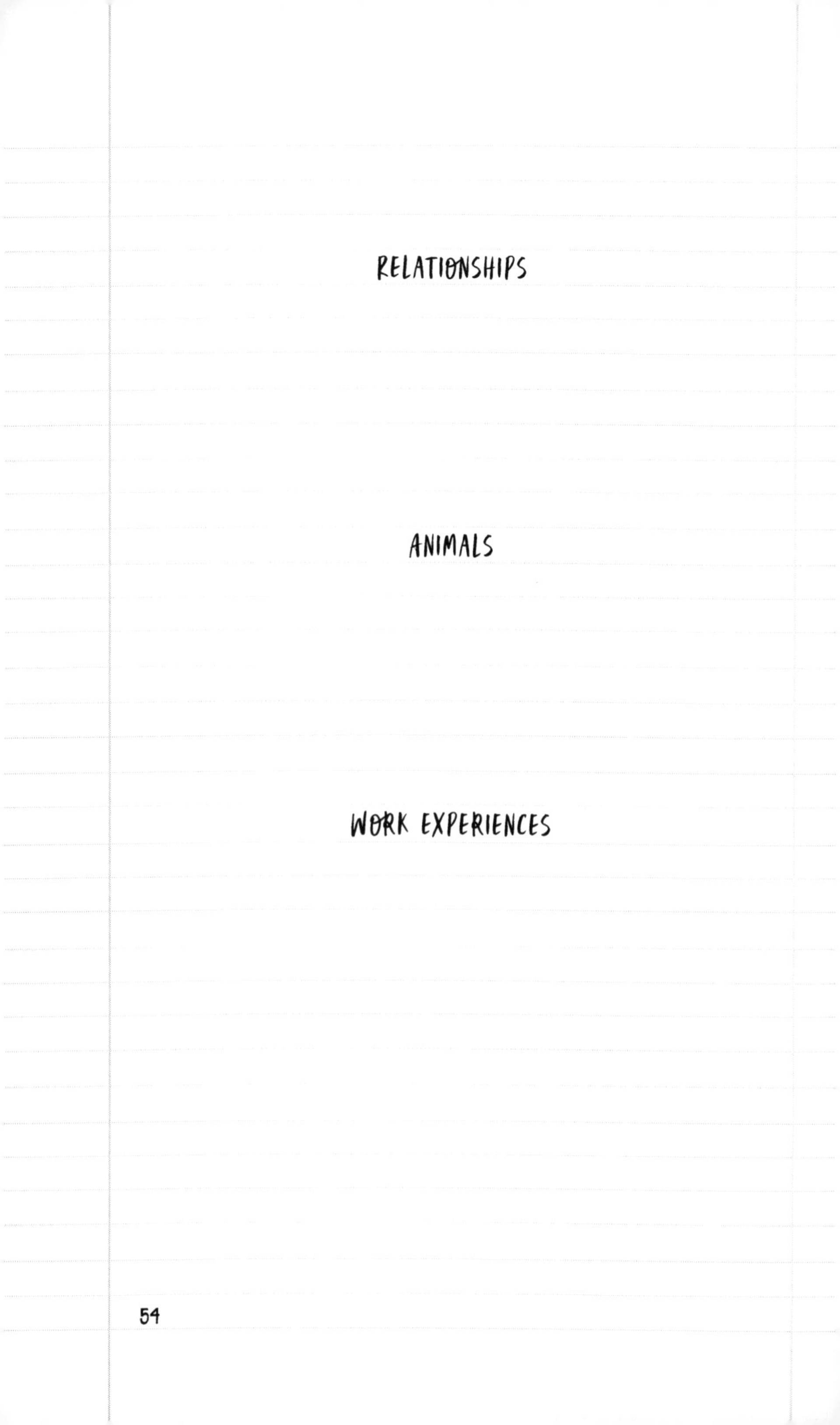
RELATIONSHIPS
ANIMALS
WORK EXPERIENCES

WRITING IS AN ACT OF PEACE

Every kind of writing connects us with our shared humanity and helps us feel and appreciate the rich complicatedness of our shared human condition.

That alone is reason enough to keep writing.

GO ORGANIC

You can think of the different stages of writing as seasons. In the same way that nature needs periods of fallow, seeding, flowering and fruiting, the writing process has its own necessary rhythm.

Every project, every writing career, needs periods of rest, as well as periods of productivity. The fallow time in writing is uncomfortable; you can't find ideas, or your ideas are not getting clearer.

If you try to push on before your ideas have firmed up enough, your writing progress will be slow and painful. If you manage to be patient, and allow the ideas to fully form up in your mind before you begin, the writing will flow.

IMPATIENCE IS A FORM
OF RESISTANCE.

IT'S GOOD TO TALK

We all need friends, and writers need writing friends. Online groups are good; organisations that run meetings and conferences where you have opportunities to meet face to face are even better. But best of all, find a few fellow writers in your area you can get together with on a regular basis for a writerly coffee/lunch/walk/drink in the pub.

If you don't know any local writers, writing courses and workshops can be a great way of meeting some. Unlike author talks and other literary events, workshops involve sharing and discussion in smallish groups, so everyone can chat and get to know each other.

Generally speaking, choose writing friends who boost your enthusiasm and energy, and avoid spending too much time with those who leave you feeling depleted.

LEARN HOW TO BE MORE CREATIVE

Most people assume you can learn the craft of writing, such as how to construct a strong plot, create interesting characters or organize your non-fiction ideas, but regard the inspiration part as largely a question of luck.

That way of looking at things is fine when it's flowing, but devastating when it isn't, because if you believe you have to passively wait for inspiration to strike, how can you be sure it ever will?

The unconscious mind is a continuous flow of images and narratives, constantly refreshed, and writers can learn techniques for dipping that stream by simply relaxing and opening their mind.

The first step is to understand these layers of consciousness, and trust in the flow.

THE FLOW IS YOUR
NATURE. TRUST
IN THE FLOW.

NOTICE YOUR MIND

Jung saw dreaming as a continuous layer of consciousness that goes on all the time, day and night, running like an underground stream beneath our conscious awareness. He said the only reason we think of dreaming as a night-time phenomenon is because most of us only become aware of it when the conscious mind is completely turned off in sleep.

If you think of dreaming in this way, you begin to notice how you naturally slip in and out of it all the time, in fantasies and daydreams. What if I go to the beach today? That person I met in the cafe last time might be there, and she might say... and then we might...

What if I hadn't said what I said? We might have gone ahead with our plan... We might be making lots of money, and then we could...

Lots of us are unaware of our daydreaming mind. It's like background noise we're so used to we hardly notice it. But for writers, conscious daydreaming – slipping between these different layers of mind – is a creative skill.

Notice your daydreaming mind today.

DREAM A LITTLE DREAM

There's a great collection of essays by writers talking about the relationship between writing and dreams, collected by Naomi Epel – it's called *Writers Dreaming*.

Stephen King describes emerging from his morning writing sessions as feeling like waking from a dream. Everyone who writes will have had that experience of being in 'the writer's trance,' so absorbed in the world of the story that the real world fades clean away.

If someone phones me when I'm in the middle of writing, I find it hard to follow the conversation because my mind is in a different mode. The creative mind is relaxed, receptive, inwardly focused, whereas the day-mind looks outward, rapidly assessing events according to the evidence of the senses and rational thought.

As writers, we have to be able to immerse ourselves in the inner world, whatever the pull of the world outside, with all its demands and distractions.

PROTECT YOUR WRITING TIME. SWITCH OFF YOUR ALERTS AND PUT UP THE 'DO NOT DISTURB' SIGN!

BREATHE IN, BREATHE OUT

The movement between the conscious and unconscious areas of the mind is like breathing in and out.

Products of the unconscious mind – inklings, intuitions, emotions, instincts and desires –emerge into consciousness, and everything you consciously know but don't currently need to focus on sinks into your unconscious mind, where it can lie undisturbed for years.

We can centre ourselves as writers by paying attention to this movement of consciousness, like meditators focusing on the breath.

READ OTHER WRITERS ON WRITING

Books by writers talking about their own personal practice and experience can be a wonderful source of reassurance. They show us we are not so weird!

That's why I've peppered this one with recommendations, and here are a few more.

- *On Writing,* by Stephen King
- *Writing Down the Bones,* by Natalie Goldberg
- *Poetry in the Making,* by Ted Hughes
- *Bird by Bird,* by Anne Lamott
- *Still Writing,* by Dani Shapiro

START QUOTE COLLECTING

What line from a book about writing have you found inspiring? Jot it down!

1.

2.

3.

4.

5.

6.

7.

8.

9.

10.

11.

12.

13.

14.

15.

16.

17.

18.

If you can't think of any, you'll find lots in the books I've recommended.

THERE MAY BE ALLIGATORS

The poet, Ted Hughes, talks about a world of imagination, memory and emotion, stories and images that goes on all the time beneath the surface, 'like the heart beat.' We may be aware of it, or we may not. We may become aware of it through writing.

Hughes compares this inner world with a pond, saying that if we don't learn the focus, patience and stealth to break into it 'our minds lie in us like the fish in the pond of a man who cannot fish.'

But you need to be brave to fish these waters. Although you might catch a tasty gorgeous trout, you might equally snare a big angry pike or a grotty old shoe. There could be alligators circling your bait, ready to pull you down.

In writing, we may find more than we might wish to find, but that is the lesson of any inner work; we are much more than what we want to be.

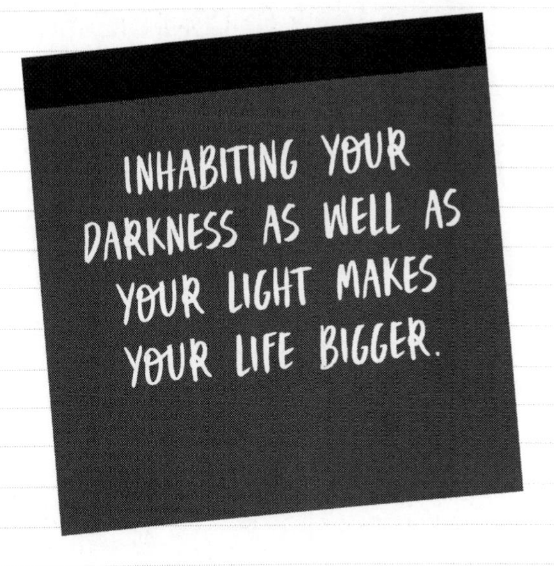
INHABITING YOUR
DARKNESS AS WELL AS
YOUR LIGHT MAKES
YOUR LIFE BIGGER.

FIND A NUMBER OF COMFORTABLE WRITING PLACES

It can be good to find other places to write besides your normal writing room. Maybe you could grab fifteen minutes for writing in your car during your lunch breaks, or take your laptop down to your favourite café when there's too much going on at home.

Two regular writing places are better than one.

'TALENT IS NOT AT ALL UNUSUAL, MY DEAR'

When I was first trying to establish myself as an author, I came upon a magazine interview with Willy Russell in which he recalled the theatrical agent, Peggy Ramsay, telling him that talent was not at all unusual; what was unusual was having the character to develop it.

I copied that out and stuck it on my study wall.

Here are four character traits I've had to work on in the course of my career:

1. Self-belief, aka a thick skin

You will struggle as a writer if you're sensitive to criticism or can't take rejection.

2. Patience

The wheels of publishing move exceeding slow.

3. Resourcefulness

Income from writing is usually low and always unpredictable, so you have to be able to find other income streams when necessary.

4. Luck

You might say, 'What's luck got to do with character?' But you make your own luck, to some extent. You have to be able to create and spot opportunities, and willing to consider any door that opens up, even if it's not one you might have considered before.

GROW!

In *The Dynamics of Creation*, psychologist Anthony Storr says many people would be surprised to learn that writers and artists, besides being dreamers, also rate highly on characteristics such as self-acceptance, dominance, responsibility, self-control, tolerance and intellectual efficiency.

I've met talented writers who would certainly be published if they had more self-belief and others, less talented, who have been published because they had the confidence and resilience to put their work out there and persevere.

Just as you can brush up on your writing skills, you can develop the character strengths you need to promote your talents through practice.

THE PSYCHOLOGICAL DEMANDS OF A CREATIVE CAREER ARE OPPORTUNITIES TO GROW.

UPDATE YOUR WRITING GOALS

As you grow through writing, new possibilities open up to you and therefore it's important to reassess your writing goals from time to time.

For example, my first writing goal was to get an agent and be published, but when that happened, it unnerved me. I wanted to write, but having books out there made me feel exposed.

So my second goal was to be a jobbing writer, taking as many writing jobs as I could, but flying under the radar. I spent three happy, productive years working for educational publishers, where they were the brand so I didn't have to be.

By then, I was confident about my writing, and able to consider developing some kind of profile, so my next goal was to write children's self-help and series fiction, which meant I had to step up and do school visits.

The experience of doing school visits gave me the courage to start teaching writing workshops and, when I found I loved doing it, that gave me the incentive to extend my practice to include all sorts of different writing organisations.

My current writing goal, to develop myself as a writer-for-writers, means I'm trying to build as much profile as I can – something I could not have imagined myself ever wanting to do when I started out.

BE MORE ZEN

Here's a Zen koan I had on my study wall for years, until it became a fundamental part of my practice. Perhaps it will also speak to you.

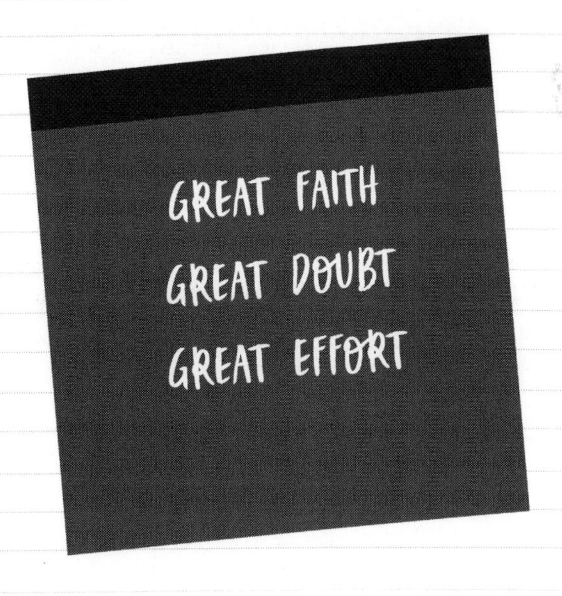

IT WILL PASS

A lot of writers suffer from low mood, and some are more prone to it than others, just as some countries are more prone to monsoon rains or winter snows. Your personality is like a climate, and your emotional states pass through you, like sunshine and showers.

Sometimes, you can feel a low mood coming on, like the dark and ominous stillness before a thunderstorm. You might not want to be stuck inside the house, or outside and soaked to the skin, but it would not occur to you to try and stop the weather.

Treat your low mood like a spell of bad weather. Batten down the hatches – it will pass.

A PERIOD OF UNHAPPY INACTIVITY IS ALMOST ALWAYS FOLLOWED BY A BURST OF FRESH CREATIVE ENERGY, IN WRITING AS IN LIFE.

HANG OUT WITH YOUR CHARACTERS

When you're writing fiction, if the plot gets stalled, quite often the problem is simply that you don't know the characters well enough.

Stop trying to work out your plot problem and get to know your characters better. Imagine meeting them in a café for a chat, or watching them as they go about their daily business.

Putting an aspect of your work in progress on the back burner – usually the structure or plot – can work just as well as taking a break from the whole thing.

HANG OUT WITH YOUR INNER CRITIC TOO

The problem with the niggling, negative voice in our head that stops us writing is that it's like background noise – we're not really listening, but it's putting us off.

If we listen and hear what the inner critic has to say, then we can argue with it.

So picture your inner critic – just the first idea that comes. Mine is often a cross little goblin, and he's got a number of things that make him cross. Not getting paid enough is one of them!

A friend told me hers was Stephen Fry as Jeeves, all snooty and superior, spouting clever put-downs.

Have a chat with your inner critic. Really listen – then persuade, argue or wrestle them out of your writing space.

Inner critics are generally more willing to go away if they know you're always willing to chat and won't try to shut them out completely.

PICTURE YOUR INNER CRITIC HERE - IF YOU DON'T LIKE DRAWING, PAINT A PORTRAIT IN WORDS

BE GLAD TO BE GREEN

One of the things I used to find inhibiting about being an author was the idea that anything I published today, I might not agree with or feel the same way about tomorrow.

So I was heartened to read John Fowles' preface to a new edition of his first novel, *The Magus*, where he says he considered making major changes to the text because he didn't really like it any more and felt embarrassed by what he now saw as its shortcomings, but he decided not to.

He saw that, unlike everyone else, writers can't censor or bury their younger selves, but that means we get to inhabit the full extent of our lives and stay, as he puts it, 'evergreen'.

FEEL CONNECTED

People think of writing as a solitary occupation but it is all about connection, whether we publish or not.

In stories, we connect with the characters we create; they come alive for us because of the way they make us feel. In non-fiction, we connect with the ideas and experiences that spark our interest and passion. In poetry, we connect with the symbolic layer of the psyche, where meaning is not objective and exact, but something the heart understands.

It's a strange anomaly that although we need to be on our own to write, in the middle of writing, we are never lonely.

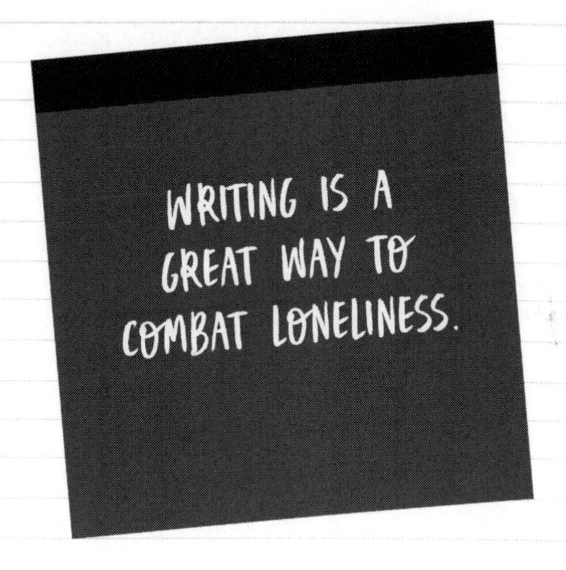
WRITING IS A
GREAT WAY TO
COMBAT LONELINESS.

GO OUTSIDE YOUR COMFORT ZONE

Trying new things is the key to living creatively because creativity is, by definition, making something that didn't exist before and when we try new things, we create brand new experiences.

Quite often, we may be reluctant to try new things – a different kind of food, book, activity or TV show – and there is indeed a good chance we won't like the new one as much as our old favourites. But if that's the worst that could happen, it's worth the risk.

It doesn't have to be a giant leap into the unknown – shaking up the little things can start a creative wave. When was the last time you parked in a different spot at the supermarket, took a different route to work, sat in a different chair in the evening, went out for a walk at a time of day when you usually stay home?

Living creatively by seeking out new experiences puts energy into all your creative work because you carry those attitudes of openness and adventurousness, and also that buzz of pleasure and excitement, into your writing or painting or gardening, or whatever creative activity delights your soul.

GOING OUTSIDE YOUR COMFORT ZONE MAKES YOUR COMFORT ZONE BIGGER.

BE NICE TO YOURSELF

It's pragmatic.

If you beat yourself up when, for whatever reason, you can't write, you'll just compound the problem with feelings of guilt, failure and self-reproach that will dig you in deeper and keep you stuck for longer.

DON'T WORRY -
YOU'LL FIGURE IT
OUT. YOU ALWAYS DO.

CLEAR YOUR CLUTTER

For a fresh burst of creative energy, there's nothing like a good spring clean. Go through the books and files that have been gathering dust unopened on your shelves, the ornaments you don't notice any more, the pictures you've got bored of, the pens that don't work and that heap of notes composting on the corner of your desk and get rid of some of them. Make some space.

It's not just about the physical objects. Clearing old notes and files means letting go of stale ideas and freeing your mind to think of new ones.

This doesn't mean you have to put them in the bin; if you think you might want to come back to them one day, just box them up and get them out of your writing space for the time being.

KEEP A NOTEPAD BESIDE YOUR BED

Try to wake slowly, if you can, not letting your mind race straight ahead to the concerns of the day.

Your unconscious will have been working away while you were sleeping, on all the preoccupations of the day, including your work in progress, and some of your best insights and ideas will come to you as you are waking up.

A notepad beside the bed sets your intention; making a decision to write your early morning ideas down means you're more likely to remember them.

HARNESS THE POWER OF THE CIRCLE

Stories naturally make circles. The protagonist sets off, achieves or learns something in the course of the action and returns changed. Often the work of redrafting is about refining the beginning and ending to tie everything into a satisfying whole. The crafting of a story is a process of perfecting the circle.

Pondering circle patterns can help you find the focus for bringing your plot full circle, and one way of doing this is by drawing mandalas. In its most basic form, a mandala is a simple circle. When you have drawn your circle, you can incorporate other geometrical forms into it and around it. You could put a triangle inside it, crossed by another triangle to make a six-pointed star. You could put your circle inside a square, or squares inside your circle. However you build your mandala, try to achieve balance, so that the sides and segments of the circle are the same.

TRY DRAWING A MANDALA HERE

Treat the whole process like doodling, not trying to create art, but simply to play and allow your mind to idle. Take your time.

COMING OUT

I often think writing is a kind of coming out; we are always revealed in what we write, whether we are aware of it or not.

Simply setting pen to paper is a self-revealing act, which may make us aware of thoughts and feelings moving through us that we were not aware of before. Certain themes that recur time and again, certain characters and patterns of relationship.

Telling other people that you write is another stage in the coming out. I've had participants at workshops who have written whole novels and never told a soul, not even their nearest and dearest.

Sharing writing with friends or family pushes this coming out as a writer a little further, as does reading to strangers in a workshop situation.

Then there's sending your work out to agents and publishers, or beta readers if you're thinking of self-publishing – people who will cast a critical eye. When you publish, the whole world knows.

Wherever you are up to, take the next step. If you write, you are a writer. Own it.

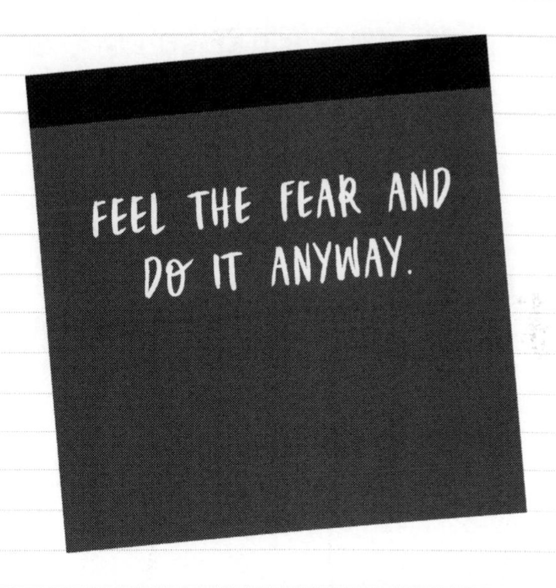

THAT'S THE TITLE OF A GREAT BOOK BY SUSAN JEFFERS - READ IT IF YOU NEED A LITTLE HELP.

REHEARSE WHAT YOU'RE GOING TO SAY

When you tell people you write, they will almost always ask if you've been published and if they should have heard of you, and your automatic response – especially if you are British – will probably be self-deprecating.

'Well, I did win a poetry prize but it wasn't one of the big ones…', 'I had a few stories in a magazine, but that was a while ago…', 'I've written a novel, but I haven't found a publisher yet…'

But, but, but!

If you've written anything at all, published or not, that's a big personal achievement. Don't just be out, be out and proud!

BELIEVE IN YOURSELF AS A WRITER IF YOU WANT PUBLISHERS AND READERS TO BELIEVE IN YOU.

CRACK ON!

When one book is finished, start straight away thinking about the next one – don't put your writing on hold while you wait for decisions from agents or publishers, or go through the self-publishing process.

Getting engrossed in new work helps to soften the blow if you get rejections and provides welcome relief from the less creative side of being a self-publisher.

It keeps the creative flow flowing.

MAKE A SEEDBED

Personal writing, such as diaries and journals, can be like a seedbed for finding new insights and ideas, as well as developing your writing voice. It can reconnect you with the pleasure of writing at times when your work in progress feels tough, because writing something no one else will ever read means you can be completely free and non critical.

Try different kinds of personal writing and find the one that suits you best, but expect that to evolve. Keeping a diary style record of your daily life might feel fun and exciting or helpful and healing during some periods, but dull and un-engaging at others.

Some people love 'morning pages', as recommended by Julia Cameron in *The Artist's Way*. Others find that such an unfocused way of working means they keep writing about the same worries and problems every day, so they prefer to work from prompts – you can find loads of those in my book, *Free-Range Writing*.

JUST START!

Here's a personal writing prompt for you. Fill this page – whatever comes, on the subject of your writing.

CONTEMPLATE YOUR OWN MORTALITY

According to philosopher, Alain de Botton, we should all start thinking about the prospect of dying from the age of about ten, because that's the best way to make sure we're putting our energies into the things we really want to do.

Then we should ask ourselves, 'What would I regret not having done if I were to die today?' Having identified our deepest wishes for our own life in this way, we should immediately make a start.

If you were to die today, what would you regret not having written?

You know what to do!

SOME PEOPLE WON'T UNDERSTAND - AND THAT'S ALL RIGHT

Writing can seem like a selfish endeavor because it takes you away from family and friends, and sometimes they may struggle to understand why you want to do it, why it's so important to you.

You may not be able to make other people understand, but that doesn't matter. In life's rich tapestry, people who like fishing will spend days sitting on a damp river bank; others who love running will spend hours circuit training, and musicians spend much of their free time practicing their instrument.

It doesn't make them selfish; it makes them who they are.

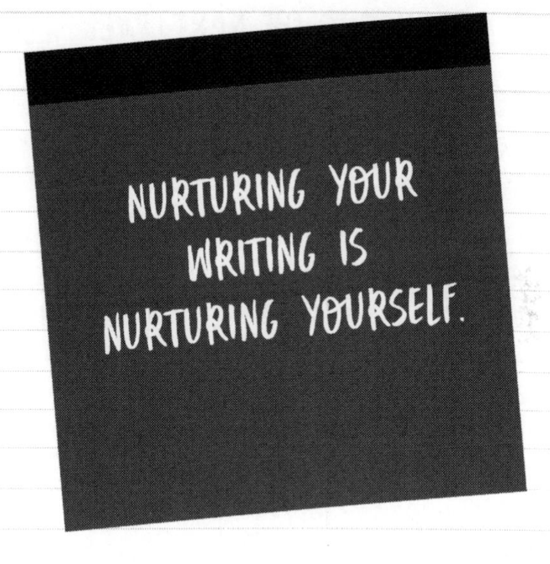
NURTURING YOUR
WRITING IS
NURTURING YOURSELF.

TAKE IT TO THE NEXT LEVEL

Why do some characters stay with you for a couple of weeks or months, and others for a lifetime? It's all about archetypes.

Your characters are first and foremost individual people with their own personal histories but at the collective level of consciousness, we all share a common humanity. People in every time and place know what it is to feel anger, pride, distress, delight; everyone has archetypal relationships, such as those between children and parents, siblings, lovers, enemies and friends.

Great stories tap into these archetypal energies. Their characters have a larger-than-life feel, because they embody more than their own personal story, making us recognise something universal in ourselves.

The grand magician when it comes to archetypal stories is William Shakespeare. King Lear is more than a foolish old King at the end of his reign – his story resonates on deeper levels, as a story of political power, in every time and place; on the deepest levels it's a story of family life and the shift in the power balance when children grow up and parents grow old.

The character of King Lear is an embodiment of an old man's folly; in the same way, Lady Macbeth seems to embody the pure spirit of ambition and Othello the spirit of jealousy.

Check out *Writing the Breakout Novel,* by Donald Maass, if you'd like to read more about taking your writing to the next level.

BE GREEDY

We live in this world as if it's our one and only life, but for writers, it nests among other lives and way beyond, stretching to infinity.

Writing is an opportunity to cross the borders into other worlds where you can be a different person, encounter new people and situations, and be changed by them, just like in this one.

If you want more adventures, more learning, more living… help yourself! When you're a writer, you can have all the lives you want.

BEING ABLE TO ROAM IN IMAGINARY WORLDS WHENEVER YOU LIKE MEANS YOU NEVER GET BORED IN THE REAL ONE.

DO THE WORK OF LOVE

A lot of people like the idea of writing, and hold it in their heart for years as 'a one day when I've got time' dream. Then, when they engage, perhaps in workshops or inspired by a book such as *Writing down the Bones* by Nathalie Goldberg or Julia Cameron's *The Artist's Way*, writing does not disappoint.

It is exhilarating to discover that all you have to do is open the door, and ideas will come pouring through. Characters, settings, stories... it's astonishing and wonderful what you find inside that you never even knew was there.

But when you fall in love with writing, just as when you fall in love with another person, your centre of gravity changes. Your instant pleasure is not the only important thing. You are willing to learn, strive and make sacrifices.

Loving your writing means:

- Working on your skills so you can properly honour the wonderful flow of ideas you have found.

- Curbing your annoying habits, such as using too many abstract nouns or adverbs, or peppering your text with one or two favourite words.

- Being prepared to give up things you really liked, such as the clever image you were pleased with that doesn't suit the voice of the piece, or the descriptive passage you toiled over that has got in the way of the action. In writing, this kind of tough love has a name; it's called, 'killing your darlings'.

Sometimes, it isn't easy, but when work is driven by love, it doesn't feel like work at all.

WRITING IS A LABOUR
OF LOVE - LABOUR
AND LOVE, BOTH.

WRITE FICTION FOR IMMORTALITY NOW

Some people say the reason they write is because they want to leave something of themselves behind. This seems a vain hope to me, in both senses of the word. Very few novelists leave works that are still read decades after they have died.

Yet, when we write fiction, we do achieve a kind of immortality, right now, because at the time of writing we are 'dead to the world', and living other lives.

BE AN ELDER, BE A CHILD

Career writers have to think in terms of sales, but the deep reason why people come to writing is more primitive and profound.

Human beings have a natural need to discover and tell their stories, not necessarily to the world, but to each other, like tribal elders gathered under a tree, or children making up games in the playground.

I think there's a natural yearning also, in such a material world, to connect with deeper layers of the self, and explore the mysteries of the inner world.

"I BELIEVE THAT IF YOU DO NOT ANSWER THE NOISE AND URGENCY OF YOUR GIFTS, THEY WILL TURN ON YOU. OR DRAG YOU DOWN WITH THEIR IMMENSE SADNESS AT BEING ABANDONED"

Joy Harjo, *Crazy Brave*

HAVE SOME FUN

Imagine you had a tail (this is an idea I heard my friend, Jen Hadfield, sometimes uses in her poetry workshops). What kind of tail would it be? How does it feel to have this tail? What can you do with it? What can it do with you?

Write about that, whatever comes. Fill up this page.

WRITING MEANS YOU CAN GROW A TAIL IF YOU LIKE. NEVER FORGET HOW AMAZING THAT IS.

OVER TO YOU

Would you like to help other writers too?

Write a note or short paragraph, like I have here – something helpful that you've read or someone's said that's encouraged you with your writing and helped you keep going when you felt despondent or stalled – and email it to me author@jennyalexander.co.uk

Mention whether you would be happy for me to share what you have written in new editions of this book, on my website and facebook page or in my newsletter, either with your name or anonymously.

IF YOU LIKE THIS
BOOK, PLEASE TELL
YOUR FRIENDS!

JENNY ALEXANDER'S OTHER BOOKS FOR WRITERS

Writing in the House of Dreams: Unlock the Power of Your Unconscious Mind is all about inspiration – where it comes from and how to keep it coming.

'An astonishing book. I don't think I've read another like it' **Susan Price, Carnegie Medal Winner.**

Happy Writing: Beat Your Blocks, Be Published and Find Your Flow is about how to keep going with a longer project or through the ups and downs of a long writing career.

'A wonderful book… wise and inspirational' **Linda Newbery, Costa Prize Winner.**

Free–Range Writing: 75 Forays for the Wild Writer's Soul will help you push your writing limits and build your skills, either on your own or with your writing group.

'Like the author's teaching style – clear, warm and full of sound advice' **Jane Moss, Host at The Writing Retreat.**

www.**jennyalexander**.co.uk

Printed in Great Britain
by Amazon